GW00496755

ROSES IN THE TEA CADDY

Dedicated to Jo and Roger, my dearest parents

The second most important command is this "love your neighbour the same as you love yourself" Mark 12.31

Join me in this second book of verse celebrating Nature and Spirit following my first collection of poems:

Let's make tea out of roses.

Sometimes life makes sense better in words and sharing thoughts and verse along the way can help get us through, bringing the warmth of spirit to our door.

Within Nature's golden wonder *"**Roses in the tea caddy**"* shares a selection of thoughts from... "Rippling along a tough sweet blend of early candlelit joy"

To "Over the drone of the hummingbird's flight..."

Enjoy the read,

Claire

Cover design by the author

Instagram: @everywordisamemory

Editor: Sharon Andrews, Instagram: @inksomnia_poetry

ONE

Agnieszka's white triangular dress
Made the world feel less of a mess
And in her veritable loud address
She put on her white triangular dress.
For if the street got busy and tired,
And if the wireless man got fired,
Before tea and if disposed
The triangular dress slipped over her toes.
So if the day clouds over with grey
And home is flagging and far away
The girl with little time to spare
Twists in a whirl of curly black hair.
And what today might well she wear?

So older now
In the evolving world
Agnieszka bright and quietly bold
Has now left her home
To be a nurse.
And at the time that tea is served
Just as the day rehearses
Her close
In her pile of new work clothes
Well heaven knows!
A crisp blue triangular dress
Starched and clean and neatly pressed!

TWO

Apple, green,
Slow, earthen
Press into the monastic flowers
Stencils of jaded love,
Un-loving the trees
That set them inside their sin,
Leaves twisting in tiger-yellow
Curls of rustling Autumn,
Colours changing,
Figs cling to bobbing apples
That turn and redden
In the garden
Of loving
And un-loving fruit.

THREE

As the mind sieves and dusts
The day-time closets of stress
A portfolio of old news
And new skill sets.
It asks piercingly
Can you help me?
In the homestead
The shadows around the orderly
Table
Lean forward, kind and able
To produce mental aid
To make the world, the moment,
More stable.
So I sieve through the dust
In yesterday's closet,
Laying to rest
The mistrust of my mind's logic
Can I forgive the man,
The ape, the conjuror,
The trickster, the barmy barrister
That let the sun burn out
And burn out again?
Cos if this means something
To anyone,
Yes.

FOUR

Avenues of sharing
Quiet skies with hedgerow,
Mountains touching
The lake's edge,
Buzzard with mouse
The seas with coral waves
The bat with cave
The moles in burrows,
The blooming trees with soapy trunks,
Kissed apples with rabbit holes,
Sharing cartwheels
Of the soul
With Winter's carol,
The avenues of sharing:
Open pathways between you and me.

FIVE

Blood-shot
And full of berries
Winter started to flower.
Her lichen gates were like rain's rust,
Over the copper grass.
Fill me with sweet holly
And carols
Bring me *mouthfuls of fruit*
Tumbling in the deep sun,
And Time's indolence,

And yes, hopefully
A lift of the latch
When Winter's work is done.

SIX

I drank my chips
And ate my beverage
The air shivered unwontedly.
The sink washed the bleach
And the bread cut the knife,
In meekness.
The days drifted woodenly
And the faeries mostly lit the way.

The reassembling mind
Kicks bins and laments
We realign our life.

The cracked compost hesitates
To renew
And garbage rebels, dented.

Kicking,
I suppose the healing waits
In sadness,
For with rusty nails the past hurt us
Knocking sins into pollution
Polluting the nails.

SEVEN

Clean wet pink puddles
Reflect the light clouds
Of the setting sun.

I finally draw the curtain,
Rest my head,
And trust the cloaked bells within.

As the shadow
Makes puddles blue,
Dreams pressed askew
Cobweb skies
Make the violet puddles new
And lift every brittle love
Subsiding in its warmer hue.

EIGHT

Deciphering your eyes
Bold tigress,
Growling in the dust.
Yellow tiger who realigned the forest,
The leafy turrets of your abode?
Bewildered you miss
The purple towers of home.
How broken is the spear of your face?
The fortress of your thunderous eye,
The lamp of lightning in the sky?
Let us reshuffle the fiery trees.
To hold and cherish thee.

NINE

Digging up mole hibernators
Like little scratches
Against a russet soil,
Blurred and hurried
Pulling,
Pressing, tightening,
Recoiling.
The gold spade,
Gravelly,
Is waiting to unwed me
From the chocolate earth
And her rich cloying
And birth is given
To the mole hibernators,
An uncluttered, satiated love
Beyond meadows,
Silken.

TEN

Don't eavesdrop on my flower
She conveys a half bloom.
Don't taste the wheat of the fields
It is half grown.
Don't listen to the ring of chatter
Not yet heard...
...But smell the swallows
In the eaves,
The wading streams,
The sun dropping like
A scarlet penny into bowls of sage
And romance.
The stars
The dreams
The flowers dangling in
The universe.
Smell the flowers first.

ELEVEN

My heart is ringed in blues
Like a dusk
Lost in reminiscence.

The flirtatious sea
Clings in incandescence.
She can bring her wave
To the happy evening sun.

I bite the grit of your dawn
The wilderness,
The wild spray.

In the early hours of rendezvous
And in moth-dew
keep the frightened wings of love
from straying
my heart is ringed in the blue
of the ocean, the reverie of you.

TWELVE

Green bark flower
Don't close the lids
Of owls, pines, snow
Dimpled on leggy darkness
Our dried feathers of gangling wings
Thud on owlish earth,
The pines,
Felled for beauty
Pour their druid hearts
Into the waves of nesting snow,
Don't close the lids,
Don't let go
Green bark flower.

THIRTEEN

Harebells
Peeped out
Of her headdress,
Sunken, as if sent away,
And raining tall flowers.

For every day
She rehearsed her return.

Full of white hooves
Of berries rolled in snow
As if pulled like reeds
From ponds of eglantine
And Freesia, she mourns.

For every day
She rehearsed her return

A flower dropped
From her petalled head
As if made from clay
And in the pond
Trees pressed
Like floating gold
Into the quiet dagger
Of solitude
Where harebells peeped out
Of her headdress,
Sunken,
As if sent away

As she rehearsed her *return.*

FOURTEEN

I carry the moon
And you flick the trees
With tigers' tails,
The ghost of copied horns
Upon bellies.
Is this love too late?
Does your fire wash out the trees,
The bluebells and bracken canopies?
Will your rapid flame
Trick the golden leaves
Of your shadow:
The tiger's ebony tattoo-
The claw of defiance?
The moon will not wane,
Will you tiger?

FIFTEEN

I scrawl the wanderings
Of my spirit
On the walls
Of the mellowing trees
That have gone yellow
Waiting for the day
I could tell you *yes*
Yes you are kind
Yes you have seen
Every twitch of human love.
You in-script back to me
On the branches of the apple tree
Yes that is true
Yes my love for you is real.
And the wind blows fast
Around my ankles
And I dwell in every shade of love
And rest in all its hues.
Yes.

SIXTEEN

I see you through pebbles
Dams, rebels of the sea.
Lonely crests crashing,
Mystics of the beaches.

I hug the ocean,
The figurative wave of slow strumming,
See the quaint untethered height
she reaches again and again
Ripples in turn fall idle
And the seagull must throw molluscs
At the shore.

Yes I see you through pebbles
Are you still fighting the tide?
I see you through pebbles,
Crushed sand between the toes.

SEVENTEEN

I see your words
Set to rhyme
And I did know
That these were the chimes
Of your love
And the songs of your heart.

Right from the start
Roses and Azaleas
Were going to line
A friendly basket
Of fruits
And we were going
To climb hills,
Share pathways,
Smile through troubles,
Remind our childhood
Of giggles
As we turn time's corner,
Through the thistles,
Forever together.

EIGHTEEN

I trace an error on thin hands
That's the cold soap

I see red veins, lingering pain
On gnarled thumbs
That's the cold soap

I see pink flamingo fingers
Bent from a wrinkled sandy wrist
That's the cold soap

I see golden hands pressed together
Lit by hope
Is that the cold soap?

I see anger, venom
Cold frightful fingers
That surely can't be the cold soap.
The cold soap.

NINETEEN

I trod on the honey-combed meadow
Sweet with clover,
Draping little lilac lobes
In the shallow grass.
Bindweed peeped like marshmallow bells
And even yellow flowers
Scattered the wilderness.
This all happened to me.
And the meadows are free.
Let the heart follow its beat patiently,
Periodically,
Through emerald greenery.
Lose the heart,
And clementine,
Honeysuckle soaked in vine
Full,
Flooded with every sense that breathes
Floating amongst the tight-veined leaves,
How beautiful
The territory that belongs to you and me.

TWENTY

In elderflower grass
The jaded sun washed
My apple filled lips with a dial of white
The day would be smashed with the moon
Of the sun.
If it was wrong to run
When tears pulled at my face
Like smarting scratches
Then my sorry tears
Will re-arrange the morning
Tracking only fragments of your voice
In the halls of vice
And your prodigy of paradise.

TWENTY-ONE

In the cold dust-grey
Of the pigeon's wing
Startling the frosted light,
Like a little lamp of suffering
Winter brings tidings
From her dwellings,
As if an evacuee
From old reminiscences.
And lowering keen spirits
Into the pensive pew
Of a doleful coo
She shields her numbness
In the cloak of Her wing.
Needing nothing and everything.

TWENTY-TWO

In the gold apricot cerise
Of the casket of leaves
Around your heavy eyes
There is a grey grimace,
A pale wince
A dark glimpse
From the trees
In their evening fleece.

there is a wilder freeze
that set twigs alight
in cold,
A stranger malaise
Than the owl can cure,
Than His marked feather can pierce.

Send the Night away,
In the gold, apricot cerise
Of her fainting leaves,
Her pale grimace
And the winter trees.

TWENTY-THREE

In the middle of the dogged dirt
You plant a lilac tree
And mark the day of her sturdy birth,
She has the bark of fleck and grey
And leans upon the garden gate.
Oh lilac peasant of the earth,
A sight of sweet and godly worth,
Rashly rinsed with purple bloom
And bringer of the afternoon.

TWENTY-FOUR

It is only a spark falling
Like the columbine
Bending to meet the earth
When her last cry is heard.

It is only your sash window,
The white paint
Reverting to yellow
As the columbine drinks
Her sorrow.

TWENTY-FIVE

It was in the summer
That you laughed into flowerpots
And set the roses straight
It was in the spring that you
Clipped the tree
Joyfully
its bloom given buoyantly.
It was in the autumn
That you swept russet leaves
From the red-stoned path
But it was in the winter
That your spade did not dig
The rugged earth
Or trespass quietly
Or tug at the weeds
That you did so love.

TWENTY-SIX

JUNIPER SNOW

If your berry were lost in the snow
The snow would smoulder,
As if tingling without a glow,
Smudged with
Yellow snowflakes, mingling
With the veil of earth,
Fallen angels in the snow.

TWENTY-SEVEN

Laughter,
Unravelling like snowfall
Threads like a glockenspiel of light
In the moon of the Night.

Beckoning the mottled blue dew,
Undoing the melancholy of your heart,
Like a sprite you season
The jangled hour
With undulating sweetness.

What a ring of innocence,
Like tubular bells
Striking each flutter
Spontaneously
Eating Cornish cream on a sunny day.

What unaltered joy
You bring
The snowfall of laughter
Echoing like jesting rivers
Less lonely,
Half dimmed autumn fruits
That we savour with delight.

TWENTY-EIGHT

Layabout leaves
Stretch in long shadow
Bridges of fixed motion,
Crawling back to
New born earth.

Surrender of sun's
Roguish light,
Clear in pointed fingers,
Her deep splashed colour
The enigma of the brightening day.

Mauve disinheritance
Of lingering blossoms
From whittled boughs
Rediscover the first seconds
Of sly glory
Rippling along a tough, sweet blend
Of early candlelit joy
And primary leaf
Where the sun lights the forest floor
And the leaves lay about.

TWENTY-NINE

Lift your heads pretty daffodils
And salute, trembling,
To soldiers
Across the meadows.
Be ladies of Spring,
Your trumpets turned up
And do not drop or lower
To the sound of fire.
Your gold has fallen into shadow
And good men are lost.
Be our glow in your row of frills
And tell us why
We cannot all be joyous
As the daffodil.

THIRTY

Like a scratch on the garden fence
A window of leopard light
On a garden bench,
trickles opal yellow
On muted grass,
Like a shaft of lily-gold
On the maple branch.
Between the crystal air
Of eventide
The collard dove
Coos
As acorns like flecked pins
Shift,
Tilting the oak,
Sunlit and muffled, adrift.

THIRTY-ONE

My heart stutters like the new snowfall,
It softly, like winter dandelion,
Lights the stars around it.
Love racing through the silver sky
Matt and still.
Roaming
The swirling hills,
Lost in time's will
How I ache to feel that new snowfall,
That trembling
The glide of feather snow
heavy on a lamp post
Tipsy and laughing,
Oh dreams lying silent,
How I long for that new snowfall.

THIRTY-TWO

Nightwatchmen
Wading in the spirit of the deep
Like a water boatman,
A lunar lid of the magic box
Full of unspoken glory,
You light and radiate the coy
Reeds and weed of tangled joy,
Not missing the locked bird
Of sorrow
Bitten in between the walls
Of the grey cage of grief.
Nightwatchman
Your tides of bee- like bodies
Fly in between different dreams
And histories
And your shadow lies unbroken
In the mass of the Night
Not yet woken.

THIRTY-THREE

Peaches lightened
By the warm rosette of sun.
plum violets against the path
of wettened mixed leaves of dun
lie in wait
of the spirit brightly wan.
Shadows hang lightly
Like octopus domes,
Grails of the apricot earth,
And Flinty skies
And every winged bird
Are lulled by the wind.
And so He flies, untied,
And every spear of sun
Grows old
On the forest floor of gold.

THIRTY-FOUR

Rinse me in rosewater
Like the plankton of the sea.
Take the *coral* out of the tea chest
And all that is not meant for me.
Fill it with tea and sea horses,
Fill it with roses,
Romances.
Fill it with dreams of the drifting mind,
The rosary I cannot leave behind.
Fill it with blossoms,
Bracken and blackcurrant weed,
Every sacred word,
The wish to be heard.
Fill it with hugs we are scared to give,
And yes , the coral
Fill it with coral
For that was not meant for me.

THIRTY-FIVE

Robin sing
To the sweet orange brown
Of the earth,
Sing where snow
May frost the frown of your eye,
Robin sing
So we may follow the trill
In the puffed throat of
Your voice.
Against the greyness of rain
May we still recall
The notes of your bright refrain
As each season
Brings your love
Right back to us again
In joy's brilliance
In the tidings of a snow
Deep within a crimson breast.

THIRTY-SIX

Roses lay before us
Sun surrendering beneath
The grip of golden leaves,
Cocoa-brown, rustling.
The roses melted
From the garden path
From waxy sculptures
Into moon shadows.
The tap of snow
Sheltered
Flower and leaf
In an igloo,
Roses lay before us.
Darkest sun,
Brightest moon
We love your roses,
Out too soon.

THIRTY-SEVEN

Speak with ears
As your garland,
blow daisies over your shoulder
As if your voice could hear the lamps
In the alleys of the skies
Tell me the way through gardens
And upside down hedges
And fish in pink rivers.
Hear me
as you speak
Did you hear me when I spoke
Of wild strawberries?
Did you hear my eyes?
Can you watch me, hear me
As you dream
Into
The yellowing sun?
Please speak with ears.

THIRTY-EIGHT

Secluded
In the drapes
Of vestments, blessed with oils
Of fresh fragrance
I ask with honesty
Do you love me ?
And within the whispered walls,
Green and blue
You say *walk with me*
And the moonlight will tell you
That my love will seclude
Every path that comes to you
And you will not fall
Because my love for you
Will not faulter.

THIRTY-NINE

The bard that crossed
The moors
Crossed,
Steady on stilts,
Inch by inch,
The gorse she beheld
It was enough.

Miles and mile
Not forgetting,
The bard *that crossed the moor*
That crossed on stilts
That crossed the gorse,
Miles and miles
Who crossed for Her,
The traveller that crossed for Her
That told her
How She crossed the moors
That dark and cold December.

FORTY

The cobbled candle flickers
Through the well of her soul
Put out like melting china.
Flowers scratch at the wax,
The wrong colour of love
Joined with the smoke
of the wrong love
the colour and the smoke
of the wrong love.

FORTY-ONE

Autumn
scuttles
in the muffled black
Berries of Night,
Withering the day's light.

In the last shadow
A jay beholds the season
Of blue wings
Her ribbon
A coloured stillness
We only find in Autumn's
Emerald ecstasy
And wilfulness.

FORTY-TWO

The larks flap above
The pale brunette earth,
Sheltering
The coppice of beauty
Where a childhood barn
Elopes to the sun.
As if the farmer and his gun
Could call us rabbits as we ran
And every day the sun it shone
For all the miles we trod and won.

FORTY-THREE

The flutter of my childhood eyes
Their soft thrill,
Laughs in my memories

Oh how those heather trees
Their waspish colour
Reinterpret my .dreams

I would not unpick those lulled hours
In evening sun
Dropping recollection in my palm

Combing through my mind
Bringing yesterday
Through time's eaglet eye
To tease my infancy
Like a fluttering moth
Round and round in moons of candlelight.

FORTY-FOUR

The moon,
The Hiawatha of the Night
Arranges her coming
Like a winter polecat.
The air stifles her blue-black.
She flies, eyeing the owlet
In the grey topaz skies

FORTY-FIVE

Christmas befalls us
Like tambourine bells.
A tree
Whispers,
Dallies, in winter cackle
Reflects back on the
Dazzled unblemished wonder.

And radiant is the silent mind
Where beauty lies
In Her matrix,
Kept like untidy leaves of
Blown away verse,
A narrative of suns,
Jingling like jasmine
Across the paths of a quiet universe.

FORTY-SIX

The sea,
Like a scaffold of Winter,
Pebble grey,
Shingle white,
Sits against a rod of silent blue,
Bluebell soft,
The gritty grey crashing waves
Splinter like the sting
Of ash-grey lily,
Galloping like a spear,
Over the heather waters,
Against the deep drone of the sea.
Unshackled shells are washed ashore
In the dimpled castor spray
In mingled flight
With bruised whistling waves,
Returning in melancholic confessions,
A farewell whispered in every greeting
As if the wash of time had ended,
Against the sleeves of silence,
Before she ever began,
Pulled back like a gentle fan
To the embryo of the sleeping
Sea strand.

FORTY-SEVEN

The soft grey whistle
Of foxy air
Dulls, and thuds with
Twilight rabbits.

The moist brunette eyes stare
On a starlit hill,
Exchange the purr of wind
For the swirling dust,
Another pair of eyes.

The simple peace
Of wet skies
Overlaps grass
With dusty wind
And gusts of dust.

Red poppies and ragwort
Thump in the gusts of foxy dust
Where wind once whistled
Through the vignette of cold
Winter thistle.

FORTY-EIGHT

The spray of the soft shandy blossom
Sparkles in the pale lily air
Rocking against the window pane.
The flower smashes through the dust of old,
And she *does reach for the small sun*
Behind the window hung
And she *does live in the breath of dreams,*
And her growth,
However young and stammered
Is clearly strong,
And she drinks as if in laughter
From the blue china saucer.

FORTY-NINE

The Summer woods
Flickered into October moss
Galloping across gold leaves
Of golden gloss.
Our hearts held in the membrane
Of the singing throat of Autumn,
Brave in the half dark
Of the wash of lavender flowers,
Half in love with the Light.
Let winter follow suit
As November recedes
Into frosty earth
Where cloudless snowdrops,
Like wands through star-dark
Seasons,
Like scanty nymphs
Bring the lime white moon
Of Spring
To her husky belonging
Thick with love's pollen
And the secrets of the infant longing.

FIFTY

The windows, half- curtained
Stir the music box of my tranquillity.
The sure frames of
Dusty yellow darkness
Waver.
The window is closed
To the sunflowers outside.
Set each curtain bright
And let the day
Stream through
Opening the music box
Of my tranquillity
Anew.

FIFTY-ONE

The winds scatter pollen
Over the drone
Of the humming bird's flight
As flickers of dusted jasmine
Are caught behind shutters
Of yellow light.

The furry bee,
Tired and droll
Packs his stockings well.

So the birds hum in swathes
Of turquoise brilliance
Now in lemon sunlight
They vanish like sorcerers
In the blank ink of Night,
As purple petals
Wrinkle in the mills of darkness
And gladness comes glowing
With every flame of joy
Its purpose
In the sun's fiery furnace.

FIFTY-TWO

My imagination
Appears like a romantic vision
In time with fogged recollection,
Of the blind furnace of my dreams.
As if in conversation with purple lilies
She watches the lullaby of waves
Roaring against the spring of shingle,
Washing back against the shore
Of bright sea spray.

FIFTY-THREE

There are sardines in my soup
The sun is peeling
Flies scratch my eyes
The curtains are stinging the skies
The grass is looking like millet
The floor is above me
The house burns its chimney
No grasshopper jumps the grass
How harsh.
In twisted beauty,
We forget, at last
Shards of sufferings
Behind the saturated windows
Of a looking glass.

FIFTY-FOUR

There goes love
Stinging my fingers,
Pinching, burning
Like mottled gold,
Rich umber.
Hushed lips,
No longer slumbering
And my memory dips
Into the husk of
My heart, thrown
Like ochre sunlight.
I resist the husks that tug
So there goes love like a cherub
blowing silver blushes in your windows.

FIFTY-FIVE

There is a butterfly blowing in the wind,
There are autumn leaves,
There are ginger wings recalling,
There is a gust of autumn scent,
The trees stumble in peacock rings,
In autumn,
Green memories,
Of the butterfly you once were.

FIFTY-SIX

There is a pattern of braid
In the tidy sky
As sinless
As the crisp rings of rainwater.

Dripping in pales
The jug flowered dunes
Of the desert-
Cobalt petals without veins
In the quiet fountain
Of open palms,
Where red stringy gnats
Tap on bricks,
And red like the rose
Of a heart in mourning
The droplets of dawn
Like a fledgling bird
Were forming
On the buttery rind
Of earth's shy gnawing.

FIFTY-SEVEN

There is the utmost joy in me
It is rising like a red balloon,
Crossing the street
And flying in gusts
Sailing over paths of dust,
Leaving behind washing lines,
A loose blouse waving
In the sunlight.
Winged in terracotta flight.
The red balloon of my heart
Wanders into the still suns
And flutters over windy trees
Tellers of deep green parks
With a shadow dance below.
Traveller of the skies
You pass us by
Like a wave of ribbon in my eye.
Pretty watcher of the sky
I let you go
To fly with pelicans.
I see you blow away
Far down the parades of singing kites
Held tight by rosy boys.
I let you go,
Blushing,
Like roses fading from my sight.

FIFTY-EIGHT

When I see the autumn acorn hats,
Damp and cracked
In the bruised shadows
I go off track
To the lavender dreams veiling my sleep.

The dark city lights
Mirrored in rainy tempestuous storms
Ignite the gloss of fascination.

It is so with hazelnuts, the dun
Tear-shaped treats,
All autumnal drinks from warm washed winds,
Trees leaning over their leaves.

It is so with sweet chestnuts
Their glow juicy, dimpled
When sun settles in a barrow of fruit,
Blows Her lingering light
To the cheeks of wandering child-sprites.

It is so when leaf-wet smells
Dally with my nostrils
And the day restlessly huddles
With the noise of starlings
And splashing puddles.

So when I see the autumn acorn
Let me go off track,
Don't hold me back
From my dappled dreams
Veiling my sleep.

FIFTY-NINE

Where are you now
Lean willow?
Laden with aching branches,
Weeping in summer dances,
Scattering floods of blossoms
Where are you now?

Where are you now
Lean willow?
In bright shadows over grass,
Quiet in hazel sunshine,
Caressing warm breezes ,
Until our sorrow slowly eases
Where are you now?

Where are you now
Lean willow?
Are your roots still searching?
Are your silver leaves bright and bursting
Are your tears no longer hurting?
Where are you now?

for Jenny

SIXTY

Why are you climbing?
There is no road here.
For there is no road here to climb,
Only the tail bone of trees,
And too tired to scale the cliffs
Of sleep
Bats flap through fires
And dragon flies fly
Like glowing wire
Over the tall trees,
A magnet of antlers
In collusion with the stars.
Lest I should take a steeper path
Bind me to the windy Nights
Where sleep is but a blink away
So there is no need to climb
Where there is no road,
Today.

SIXTY-ONE

With this paddle I give you
The fins to cross the sea.
With this boat I give you the map
To the rose garden of my heart.
With this anchor I give you the rock of trust
To keep you on course.
With these words I give you
The verse of love.
Sailor of waves and coloured fish,
Nautical dolphin,
Set sail
And join the seas
With the blood red sky
Where crystals jump
Over clouds like whales,
Moon-bathing,
And lost in the sea's curls.
Join me
Ever one with the sea.

SIXTY-TWO

You can be a friend of time,
Biting at her heels,
Blowing mimes at the wind,
Blowy
Through the crimson air,
The blowy, kind , familiar
Taste of spiced wind
Billowing into an endless cloak
Of time.
You can be a friend of time
And through the bend
Of her ghostly pining
You can be a friend of the winds of time
secret scents blown sideways
through a timeless bottle,
wind and time like a daisy chain
of tiny hands blowing daisy clocks
like bubbles,
Time and wind in a spin,
Never forgetting which way the wind blows
And where they both begin.

SIXTY-THREE

Are these words of love?
So let the heather gills
Soothe my sea,
faith
A pretty gorse growing
standing like coral
Her gills,
filling the air of the moor,
once grey,
Now in conversation with the sun,
Mauve bay, and studded shore.

Printed in Great Britain
by Amazon

16444391R00041